T0120619

Life with an AVM

Grace Mary Fernandez-O'Brien

BALBOA.PRESS

A DIVISION OF HAY HOUSE

Balboa Press books may be ordered through booksellers or by contacting:

Balboa Press
A Division of Hay House
1663 Liberty Drive
Bloomington, IN 47403
www.balboapress.com
844-682-1282

Print information available on the last page.

ISBN: 978-1-9822-7219-7 (sc)
ISBN: 978-1-9822-7220-3 (e)

Balboa Press rev. date: 06/13/2022

Contents

Appreciation to the Value of a Miracle

Strength does not come from physical capacity.

It comes from an indomitable will.

Live as if you were to die tomorrow.

Learn as if you were to live forever.

— Mahatma Gandhi

Nothing ever happened in the past,
that can prevent you from being present now.

— **Eckhart Tolle**

Introduction

Childhood is usually a time in life where you don't know about anything that might be wrong or anything that could be dangerous. For many, it's a time when Mom, Dad, and family take care of them and keep them safe and well. If a child does not feel well, it's usually noticed, as a child will cry and appear weak. As the child grows, the child can let family know he or she is not feeling well and ask for assistance. Unfortunately, at times, children feel ill in ways they had not before. That can make a child fearful and unable to express what he or she is experiencing.

I was born on August 20, 1971. I was the third child my mom conceived, but I was the second one to live. Her first child was unfortunately a miscarriage. My father was an only child. His mother had lost three children at birth. No one really knew the reason for those losses. Back in the 1920s, 1930s, and 1940s, when my parents were born and raised, there were not many ways of knowing why you had just lost a child. This was especially true in the part of Spain where my family had started. There we many deaths in the family; both of my grandfathers died young, and there were many more. Stories of past family instances sometimes made me understand what might have been passed down to me without anyone ever even knowing about it. I feel the illness was finally noticed, late in my family's life, in me.

Chapter One

When I was young, I remember being with my father in the living room while he watched TV. I loved to make things from scratch. While he rested on the couch, I would be at the end of the sofa, in a small space up against the wall, making a dollhouse with construction paper and tape. I would start the length of the dollhouse from the sofa and attach it to the wall. Then I would let my dolls play in it. When the weight of the doll would break my house, I would become upset. I remember getting a headache from the stress of watching the paper dollhouse collapse after having spent so much time on it. My father would lay me down with him on the couch to watch TV until my headache was gone and it was time for dinner.

When I played with my dolls, I spoke to them as if they were my friends. We would walk around the apartment and be in another world. I would have conversations with them, and they always responded to me in my mind. But sometimes while having a conversation with them, I would get a headache and feel like my dolls looked blurry. I would then hug the dolls as hard as I could until the feeling went away.

While carrying my toys from one room to the other, or just walking into the kitchen, I would walk straight and suddenly start leaning sideways. I sometimes bumped into the doorway on my way. My grandmother would tell me to look up and pay attention to where I was going. The only problem was that I knew I was paying attention; I just didn't know that dizziness and blurriness were about to happen. I tried explaining that to my grandmother, but she told me I was just not being observant of what was in front of me. I would complain about the headaches and dizziness, but I was told they were from being so skinny and not having enough food in my body to keep me strong. My grandmother was my best friend. I love and miss her so much! She lived with us and watched my siblings and me while my parents were at work.

My brother is five years younger than I am, and all we did as kids was fight. He would follow me everywhere. He would play outside with me, and inside as well, but would not leave me alone. I would get mad at him, feel dizzy, and have a headache. My grandmother continuously said it was from not having enough food energy to keep me from headaches. My mother asked the pediatrician why I was so skinny. He said I should take vitamins to keep me strong and prevent sickness. I remember those vitamins were bigger than I was!

I'll never forget the day I was playing on the kitchen floor while my mom was cooking dinner. I played a lot in the kitchen with her and loved helping her with dinner. But one day I got very dizzy again, and this time I felt nauseated. My head started to hurt, and I wanted to yell out to my mother, but I could not get my mouth to function. I tried moving my arms to get her attention, but I was unable to. I sat on the floor with my doll, listening to her talk, but I could not move or respond; I just watched everything spin and felt pounding in my head. When it was finally over, I got up but felt very weak. I could hardly hold myself up. I asked my mom to hold me in her arms. I was so scared. I couldn't remember ever having such a scary episode. This was not the first time it had happened, but it scared me to that extent because I was unable to move. It was as if something was holding me down.

My mom asked what was wrong when I wanted to quicky be in her arms. I told her I wasn't feeling well but did not know how to explain it; it was as if my thought for speech was gone. I couldn't explain it because I was unable to think correctly, and my words were trapped in my mouth. What I was thinking just would not come out. My mom fed me and gave me my milk before bed. She was nervous because I didn't have enough energy in me. She took my temperature, but there was no fever; therefore, I was okay. My mom was a hardworking woman taking care of family. She was always there to be sure we were well, but situations like this were hard for me to describe. I didn't even know what had just happened.

Chapter Two

One ne day in kindergarten, I was asked to complete a math activity worksheet, and I was unable to. I was 100 percent blank on how to complete it. I will never forget that day. The teacher was upset with me and did not allow me to leave for lunch until it was complete. I felt dizzy, could not even understand anything being said to me, and was scared, having forgotten where I was. The teacher thought I was ignoring her. They asked my sister (who was in eighth grade) to come pick me up and take me home. They said I was not paying attention and refused to do the work. I told my sister I tried to do what was asked, but I could not remember any of it. I didn't know why. I was afraid to go back to school. I was afraid of getting in trouble for not completing my work, but at the same time, I was very frightened of what was happening. I continued feeling dizzy and unwell for the rest of the day.

Those episodes happened many times and were never noticed by others. One day in gym, I was playing with the girls on mats doing cartwheels, and I kept getting dizzy and falling. I loved gymnastics but didn't understand what was happening. Some girls even said I was no longer as good as I thought. I told my teacher that I felt dizzy, but no one took care of me. The teacher and the other students must have thought that I was lying about having headaches and wanted to leave class. If I was sent to the nurse's office, the nurse would tell me that, like it or not, I was not going home. On the days I did have a fever, they would still make me stay, saying I always tried to leave.

I then started to hide my headaches and dizziness because I did not want to get in trouble. One day in fifth grade, I was asked a question by the teacher and was unable to answer. Again, I was very dizzy and had a hard time responding. She was upset with me and made me sit in the hallway for the rest of the day. I was very upset. I told her I didn't feel well, and she said I looked fine.

I felt I wasn't liked in school. Even the kids in my class would laugh at me for being sent to sit in the hallway. That year, I was even held back. The only person I felt liked me and felt for me was the principal, Sister Eileen. She was always very nice to me. However, I was afraid to tell her what I was experiencing because I didn't want to lose that friendliness. Toward the end of my grammar school years, through seventh and eighth grade, Sister Eileen asked me to help out in the convent on weekends. I helped clean the sisters' rooms, the kitchen, and the chapel. Doing that helped me with some of my grades. I still had trouble with one class in particular because the nun who taught that class was very upset with me.

It was a Saturday, and there were no kids in the school and no one else was around, except me. While looking through the school window from the outside in, I thought I saw someone in one of the classrooms. As I kept looking, I noticed a nun making out with the janitor. I was appalled! Unfortunately, I was also in trouble. The nun told me that if I said a word, I would not graduate. She even failed me and made me do summer work. Funny how things were when I was a child; we always got in trouble regardless of who was at fault. I never told Sister Eileen what happened.

By the end of grammar school, unfortunately, my father had passed away. Because he'd been in the hospital for so long and the family was always being asked to come see him quickly, I missed a lot of classes in school. I was almost held back again in eighth grade. It's a good thing Sister Eileen cared so much for me. She let me do work at home during the summer of my eighth-grade year. She actually spoke to the sisters of Holy Family Academy, asking them to let me enter as a freshman. She told them that my grades were only low because I'd lost my father. I spent a lot of weekend time on convent work, and although I had many headaches and dizzy spells, it did help me.

One day, while having a hard time concentrating, I cried and said a prayer to my father to please help me finish the work I was given. I trusted and always felt his presence, and was finally able to finish. When I gave all the work in, completed, they were proud of me. They told me they knew I was smart and would have no problem. I was then sent to Holy Family Academy for my freshman year of high school.

Chapter Three

I used to ask friends if the things that were happening to me ever happened to them. They all said no and thought it was funny. They felt I was always being silly and liked making people laugh. Also, when I was getting really mad about something, I would automatically get dizzy and lose my balance. Again, I asked my friends, "Doesn't that happen to everyone?" But they said, "No, Grace only you!"

Another time I remember falling to the ground two times while being dizzy was during a school dance. We were all there ready to dance and have fun. The girls would be closer to the front, already dancing, while the boys were standing in a group just watching. I loved to dance, but both times that I stood by the disco lights, the room started spinning and I fell to the floor. I kept trying to get up but would lose balance and drop. I was embarrassed, but I also felt something was wrong. I mentioned it to one of the parents there and that parent just said some lights make some people dizzy. My classmates thought I was being funny again, but in reality, I almost sat during the whole dance. I was frightened to try and dance with those lights flashing. I had no idea what was happening. It was as if I was being controlled. I thought this must happen to others, but whenever I asked people if it ever happened to them, they kept saying no. It kept me wondering why me? That night after the dance, I walked with friends to the Broadway Dinner. They all said I was being silly by falling to the ground. They all thought I was being myself and trying to make others laugh. I gave up saying I was dizzy, convinced no one would believe me.

On days I would be outside hanging out with my friends, I sometimes had episodes with dizziness, but in milder forms. We would be playing hide and seek, and from running and trying to not be found, I would become dizzy. We would play in the dark and hide in other people's backyards. Having a dizzy spell at that time was weird; I could come out of it and forget where I was hiding. I would be caught many times, since I walked out of my hiding spot to see where I was located. I would try to explain it to my friends, and they thought I was being ridiculous.

At times, after having an episode while sitting with other people, I was unable to answer a question or remember the simplest story that should have still been in my short-term memory. I would tell the story I had in my head, but I would be called "Theory" because I told the wrong version. I didn't know how to describe what was happening to me, and the times I did, no one believed me. Whenever I tried to explain, I was told I was going crazy, and that what I experienced doesn't really happen to anyone. I would run to my grandmother, or my mom, to tell them I was dizzy, but I was always told I needed to eat or perhaps I was dehydrated.

Chapter Four

A s I got older, the symptoms began to change. Accompanying the episodes of dizziness, headaches, loss of memory and movement, I began to remember and even hear voices of people from my past. I would very often have a memory of perhaps a TV show or of a day in my toddler years. When I would try to remember it more, I would quickly have an episode. Sometimes I would hear the voice of the person I was thinking about, like the women from *The Magic Garden*. I would hear them singing the show's song "It's nice to say hello, hello, hello and how are you." I would try to remember the show and get dizzy. The sound of *The Magic Garden* was very loud, not a whisper. When I would tell my family, they couldn't believe that I remembered things from so long ago. They thought I was just having normal memories.

I amazed my mother by telling her about things that happened when I was a toddler. I mentioned times that had passed, and I was told by family and friends that there was no way I could remember those things. My mother was always so surprised that I had memories from so long ago. She thought it was amazing I could remember such events. Some things I remembered were conversations she had with my father or grandmother long ago. I remembered talks I had with my father. I also remembered the conversations I had with my great Aunt, Tia Baltasara. She told me stories of my father when he was a child. I would play with my cousin at her house and I loved sitting down to hear the stories. Of course, as I grew up, I forgot many of them, but during an episode I could sometimes hear her voice. The problem was that I was unable to explain what would happen to me as those memories came to mind. I would again be dizzy with a headache, and my thoughts were loud in my head. At that point, I decided I might need to see my doctor.

As a young woman, I was always very thin and involved in sports, dance, and gymnastics. For some reason, my strength and breathing became weak. I would lose strength and not be able to breathe correctly. That, too, would bring on dizziness. Although throughout my life, I could eat anything and stay slim, my weight started to climb, and I felt weak. When I described to my doctor some of the episodes I was having, including the new ones of weakness and difficulty breathing, the doctor said I was stressed with school and needed to go the gym and take more care of myself physically. My weight increased quickly—eighteen pounds in one summer. I was very weak and still experiencing episodes, so I decided to join the gym and try to relax. I had never been to the gym, because I was always underweight. After gaining eighteen pounds, I was at a more normal weight for someone my age. If anything, I started looking more normal to some people instead of being so bony, as I always was. But it still was not me.

When I started going to the gym, I used to walk on the treadmill and feel weak. When I lifted weights, I had to quickly put them down. I swam and tried to relax in a sauna. but unfortunately, I could not relax. Not too long before that, my father had died of cancer, and I started thinking I had perhaps inherited an illness. I looked online at symptoms, and thought that there was a possibility that there was something wrong with my thyroid. I once again visited my doctor and as usual, my doctor thought I was being paranoid and told me to calm down. But I couldn't.

I quickly started having frequent anxiety attacks. I returned to my doctor, and demanded he check me for these illnesses. My blood test results revealed that nothing was wrong. Everything they checked for came out negative, and they said I was healthy enough not to worry. I was told that I was too fearful and was looking for ways to draw more attention to myself. I knew that was not the case. I felt I was being given signs that something was wrong with me. I had been feeling strange things ever since I was a child. My sister was a nurse, so I decided to read through all her nursing school books to try to find my symptoms. I knew there was something medically wrong with me, but I could not find out what it was. I found nothing, and no one understood what I was going through. I felt I had no choice but to learn to accept my symptoms. I also thought that perhaps something like this might be happening to more people than just me, and that things might be okay…perhaps.

Chapter Five

⁓⸙⁓

I had already gone through difficult high school years, since my father died so young right before freshman year. During my sophomore year, I had to change from the Catholic high school to the town's public high school. This was not my choice. I was asked to leave. I wasn't at all a bad student, but I feel I wasn't well liked by one of the teachers. I learned that the hard way.

When I started my freshman year and signed up for a Spanish class, the teachers thought that, since I was fluent in Spanish, I should take the junior/senior Spanish class. I didn't feel too good about that. They told me that if I felt uncomfortable or didn't feel it was good for me, I should let them know and they send me back to freshman Spanish. I did ask them to send me back many times, but they refused.

I felt like the Spanish teacher did not like me. Perhaps he was unhappy that they sent a freshman to his class. When we read chapters out loud, starting from the first student sitting in the front of the class and going back one by one, he kept skipping over me and going to the next student. He said I already knew Spanish and didn't need to be part of reading out loud. When we had tests, he failed me by one point. I would ask him why I failed, and he would make up something like "You spelled this wrong." I always felt like telling him that I *did* spell it correctly, in proper Spanish, because the book we were studying from was written in Mexico, not Spain.

I was flabbergasted on the last day of the year when we received our report cards before we left for the summer. I saw that I failed Spanish again by one point. Being so angry made me dizzy, and I held on to my desk, feeling like I was going to fall. The room was spinning and my head started to hurt. Crying, I rushed to get some water and then I finally got my strength back. Strength led me to the Spanish teacher's office to say, "How can you fail me?"

His response was, "Well I guess your Spanish isn't as good as you thought."

I replied, "Really? Pues tu eres gordo y tambien eres un pedazo de mierda (in English: You are fat and also a piece of shit). How was my Spanish there?" Unfortunately, he wasn't very happy. I was then asked not to come back to that school in September.

A year later, the administrators at the Holy Family Academy called me, asked for my forgiveness, and asked me to return. I was still upset at them for making me take the Spanish class, even though I didn't want to, and then being treated poorly by the teacher. I decided to stay in the public school, Bayonne High School.

It was hard to settle in with new friends, having been separated from previous ones, but that was okay. I met new friends in school, as well as a childhood friend who lived next door to me growing up. She would always be around. I had a tough time studying for some tests, but I was passing my classes, fortunately. I would always say a prayer to my father to please help me study because I always had a hard time. Everything I tried to memorize would disappear. I would make songs with the information I wanted to learn in order to pass a test. I chose a song I liked and just changed the lyrics. During my tests, I would sing myself the song with all the facts, and that astonishingly helped me pass. From there, I was able to graduate and start anew.

When high school was finally over, I wanted to go to college. I had always wanted to work in a career involving American Sign Language (still do). I remember as a young child, I was at McDonald's once with my mother. On Saturdays, as long as I was a good girl in the supermarket, my mother promised to take me there for lunch. While waiting in line one day, I saw a child talking to his mother in sign language. That was the first time I ever saw sign language, and I was inspired. From then on, I started teaching myself sign language.

I looked forward to evolving with it, but I was having a hard time just getting through the start of college. I wound up attending five different colleges and not passing one full year in each. I was having a very hard time studying. I would spend a lot of time trying to study and be prepared for a test, but then I would freeze and fail almost every time. In college, teachers would ask me test questions in person, and I would know the answers. When I would sit to complete an exam on paper, I would be too stressed to remember a thing.

I even took a psychology class to help me learn to study and take tests, but although I did learn a lot, it didn't help. The class taught us to close our eyes before the test and take deep breaths and clear our minds of nervousness and be calm. That was supposed to help us concentrate more on the information we had studied. I might have been the only person in class looking like I was meditating. I still kept feeling dizzy and lightheaded every time I sat to take a test, even with meditation. I kept trying new colleges, but that didn't help. I was so upset at myself, thinking I wasn't able to study hard and pass with a good grade. My sister had graduated college and became a nurse. My cousins were in college, as well as my friends. Why couldn't I be like them? I finally gave up college.

Without knowing which way to go, and needing the money, I started working in the hotel business. I was there for years. I started feeling a little better, showing that I was smarter than I previously felt I was. The hotel business even transferred me to Buffalo, New York. They trusted me with accounting. It was something I was always good at. I would get calls from other hotels asking me to assist when their managers were out for the day or night. I was trusted at many properties. I was even in training to become a manager.

Chapter Six

*L*ife continued, and although nothing much had really changed, I was able to fall in love and get married. I also decided to join the New York Society for the Deaf and learn sign language. I loved my sign language course. It was once a week in Manhattan. I felt I was able to speak sign language very well. But when we were tested on signing in public, I would again get dizzy and not be able to communicate. I was upset. I didn't understand why I would just forget things and then know them again once the test was over. I started feeling that I wasn't as smart as I had thought. After many years in the hotel business, I was offered a new job in a corporate office—the type of job I said I never wanted. It paid more money, so I accepted. What I had in mind was always working with children using sign language. But I started in corporate, and I am still here today. I still wish I could have completed college to have the career I dreamed of as a child, but I am grateful that I work with a good group of people who teach me and allow me to be myself…sometimes.

Early in marriage, I was pregnant with my first child. While pregnant, I would be on the train to work in New York City, standing the whole way, and feeling swollen by the time I was at my desk. I sometimes looked down on my desk and saw blood on my papers. I had constant nosebleeds and dizziness. Although my episodes continued, I had a good overall pregnancy and gave birth to a healthy baby boy through C-section. I wasn't very happy that it had to be a C-section, because I wanted to have a natural birth. My doctor had plans to go away on vacation, and he couldn't wait any more for me to give birth naturally. He said a C-section would be better for all of us, and so we did.

Of course, with most pregnancies, there is always a little bit of pressure. Mothers tend to put their own lives aside to care for the most important thing in lives: their children. But even as a busy mom spending all my time with my baby boy while on maternity leave, I was still having episodes. My first son Shawn was colicky, and would be up crying until late into the night. I remember holding him late at night and feeling dizzy. I thought it might only be from lack of sleep. I one time had him in my arms and I started feeling the room spin. I held him tightly so I would not let go, and I fell backwards. I was lucky that the stove was right behind me and it stopped me from landing on the ground. At one point, I was even afraid to be left too long alone with him. I was afraid something would happen to me and I would have no help.

When Shawn stopped being colicky, I was able to return to work. Shawn brought nothing but smiles to all of us, but my episodes still did not end. I lived with shortness of breath, dizziness, and headaches. On Christmas Eve one year, we were at my mother-in-law's house to celebrate with relatives. When family came up the stairs, they stopped and greeted us all with hugs and kisses. Suddenly, I felt something happening to me. As I was being spoken to and hugged, the room began to spin. I had a really bad headache, was dizzy, and could not get a word out of my mouth. I could not even move. I was so scared, I didn't know what to do. I felt I was being trapped. I thought I was going to fall off the stool, but I tried holding on to the counter. I didn't have any strength, but it did help. I then started thinking to myself, *Stop, stop, stop* repeatedly, until it finally worked, and I came back to normal.

That was one of the same feelings I would get as a child. While I would be out with friends, laughing or meeting new people, I would freeze the same way I did at my mother-in-law's. It had been a while since the experience was that strong.

I kept a smile on my face while people were talking, and not one person noticed what had just happened. When I finally came to, I had to get up and sit on the couch to relax. I still had a headache and had no idea what had just occurred. I never was unable to speak or move during my adult life. I thought things like that ended when I was a child. I was terribly frightened.

Chapter Seven

I went back to the doctor and told him I was still feeling the same way, and even worse. He told me I was suffering from post-partum depression. I told him I had been feeling this way before I had my child, and I did not think that was the issue. He then told me I should spend more time out with my friends, go out to dinner, and so on. He said I was spending too much time alone at home, or stuck with my child and not having an adult to talk (my husband was at work longer than me). I therefore gave it a try.

I joined a yoga class with a few of my friends. I loved yoga I was even taking classes to one day teach yoga. (I wanted to give yoga classes at Memorial Sloan Kettering to cancer patients. Soft yoga with meditation is very helpful for patients and all others.) My friends and I would always have fun at yoga class. Perhaps because we had known each other since we were children, we knew how to be silly and laugh throughout the class. We had to stop going to that yoga studio, because we kept getting in trouble for laughing all the time. Everyone had his or her eyes closed while in a relaxing pose, but then one of us would make a noise that had us all laughing. It was embarrassing to act that way, but sometimes, regardless of your age, when you are with childhood friends, you are reminded of the times you had with them as children.

I was glad we were leaving on the last day because, while we were there, I had another episode. We were all standing upside down against the wall and as I got down from my pose, I was dizzy again with an unbelievably bad headache; I felt like I could not communicate. I did not want to be noticed, so I closed my eyes and kept repeating to myself *Go away, go away*, until it ended. I had to quickly step away from my friends before they noticed I was unable to move. Then I was stuck, frozen, and very frightened. I finally came back and just wanted to go home.

I once again retuned to my doctor and explained what had happened. He said, "Things like that sometimes happen after childbirth when some moms are stressed and feel their lives are no longer ones that people are interested in. Some think they are sicker than they are to get more attention to make them feel better!"

I could not take it anymore. I gave up. No more doctors. I decided to take a different approach. I spoke to other types of professionals and was told that perhaps since I was having thoughts from so long ago and hearing voices, that I might be repressing something from my past. They said something, like molestation, might have happened to me as a child and, although I did not consciously remember, my thoughts were still there. One person even told me that I might be inhabited by a spirit that wished to speak through me. Although they could have been correct, once again, I gave up. I would just have to deal with whatever was wrong with me; no one could help. I was even afraid to let anyone know. I was too embarrassed by it.

Chapter Eight

*F*ive years after my first child was born, we had our second child, Anthony. I wanted to try to have him naturally, but he too had to be born through C-section. My gynecologist's son was going to do a C-section with Anthony for his first time. When Anthony was born, pictures were taken and everyone was so happy, not just Patrick and me as parents, but both doctors as well. Anthony was a little different from Shawn. He would fall asleep more easily. On weekend mornings, in order to not wake up Shawn, I would take rides in the car with Anthony to help him fall asleep quicker, when needed. We would ride to the park or just around town.

Unfortunately, I would sometimes have slow starting episodes that would make me pull over to call a family member and talk, just to get my mind off what feelings I was starting to experience.

Those feelings were dizziness and headache. I would many times stop and call my mom to have a conversation. That way my mind would overpower the feeling that was starting and that scared me so much. It was as if I learned to control and stop the episode I was about to have before it occurred. By changing my train of thought, the dizziness and headache would stop happening. I would sometimes raise the volume on the radio and just start singing to the song that was playing. That always seemed to help. Although I knew there was something wrong, and I felt that later in life I would suffer the consequences, there was nothing else I could do. No one understood what I was feeling, and I no longer had anyone to talk to about it.

One day, I was driving with Anthony in the car to the mall, a place I knew exactly how to get to, and I had those feelings again. All of a sudden, my mind went blank, and I did not know where I was. I quickly pulled over and looked around to see if it would come back to me, and it would not. I picked up the phone to call my mother, but I could not remember her number—a number we had since I was six years old. I tried to call my husband, but I could not remember his either. I started singing to try to fight it, but this time it won. I was lost on a road I knew well, and I could not think where I could be. That was the worst moment ever. They were new feelings that I had never felt before. My head was spinning, I was very frightened, and I feared for our lives. After perhaps ten or fifteen minutes, which seemed like forever, I recognized where I was and was able to drive back home. In a panic, I thanked God that my son was sleeping, and I was able to get through this without getting us hurt.

When I got home, I tried to explain to my husband what had happened but was unable to explain myself clearly. No one could understand what I went through. I almost stuttered and could not speak the words I was thinking to describe what had just happened. After that episode, I was in fear.

Less than a week later, I developed a fever and needed to see a doctor to write me a prescription. This time, I decided not to go to the doctors I had been seeing in the past, since they might have told me the fever was from post-partum depression. I asked my husband to help me find a new doctor and he recommended a doctor he had just recently heard of: Dr. Ellen Black. I quickly made an appointment. As I sat in the examining room waiting for her to see me, I thought to myself, *Should I tell her what happened to me? Is she going to think I am psychotic? Or that I might have a mental illness? Should I explain all my endless experiences?*

When she came into the room and finished examining me for my fever, I took a deep breath and said, "Dr. Black, please don't think I have a mental problem and want to be placed in a psych ward. Also, please don't think I am being inhabited or repressing some memory. I need to explain what is happening to me, I am afraid, and I cannot take it anymore."

After I went through my life story, she looked at me with a concerned face and said, "Grace, I don't think you're crazy. I think you're having an epileptic seizure." I had no idea what she was saying, but I did recognize the word epilepsy. That made me scared, but it didn't matter to me. I was so grateful that someone finally had an answer. She then scheduled me for an MRI. I anxiously and, believe it or not, happily went for an MRI that would take half an hour. My then husband, Patrick, accompanied me and sat in the room where he was able to see me through a glass window. I realized when the radiologist kept telling me, "Just a little while longer" that I had already been there two hours longer than what was scheduled.

When we finally left the office, my husband described to me the faces that were made while they performed the MRI. He said the radiologist called in another person and they looked at the pictures together. At one point, they were on the phone with my insurance to be able to continue taking pictures. He also said they looked nervous while doing so. They were looking at my brain like it was something they had never seen before. That was a scary thought to me. *Do I have cancer? Might I have been right years ago and they finally saw a tumor? In my brain?* I was very frightened not knowing what could be giving me seizures.

Two hours after that visit, as I was waiting for my son to come out of grammar school, I received a phone call from Dr. Black with results from the MRI. I was told that I had an AVM, arteriovenous malformation, in my brain. I never heard of that and asked her to please spell it. I also asked her if it were life threatening or curable. She explained that an AVM in the brain is not cancerous, but it happens at birth; while the veins and arteries are forming, they combine and form a knot. The knot then traps blood, keeping it from circulating within my veins and forming an AVM, which is almost like a bubble. The malformation was nearly two and one-half inches in size. She was very honest and told me that since it was such a rare illness, she did not know the answers to my questions. She had looked it up before calling me to tell me what she had read. She gave me the name of a doctor in Bayonne who might know more about it. He was a neurologist and she felt he might be familiar with AVMs.

Being in shock, I continued to wait for my son coming out of school and was in a weird type of awe as I walked home. I had a hard time knowing what to think. *Am I glad something was found? Am I scared? Will I be a lost mother to my children? What is happening to me? Why me?*

Chapter Nine

I quickly made an appointment to visit the neurologist in my town and Patrick accompanied me. When we showed him the MRI and what I had been told was my illness, he went to his office to review the diagnosis. We waited over an hour before he came out to tell us that, in his ten years of practice, he had only seen two people with an AVM, and unfortunately neither had lived due to hemorrhages. He stated that I should accept what I had and just enjoy the life that I would be able to continue living, for most of the time it is incurable. He also mentioned it is rare and no cure has been found for it. He stated I could die today or live a few more years until it decided to rupture.

Patrick and I left the office with tears in our eyes. Patrick was supposed to return to work after my appointment, but he was too devastated to return. He called work and asked to take the rest of the day off to come home with me. My husband and I left the office full of fear. I sat and thought of nothing more than my children and how their lives would be if they lost their mother so early. I always knew there was something wrong. I went through life feeling it, but I was never able to get help or even be understood. There must be something that could be done.

When I mentioned the news to my family members, they were all in shock, especially my mother. My sister-in-law at that time told me that, when the mother of a friend of hers had an aneurysm, she had seen a doctor from New York who was said to be one of the best, and she gave me his name. Then my cousin, who is a radiologist in New York, mentioned the same doctor's name, and I then knew where to go. The doctor they were both speaking of was Dr. Alejandro Berenstein at the Hyman Newman Institute for Neurology and Neurosurgery in New York.

We nervously scheduled a meeting with him and Dr. Joon Song, who was a part of his group and the one who would take over my case. I arrived at the hospital for my appointment and was extremely nervous. *What if I don't make it home? What if the neurologist was right and I am not going to live through this?* Upon seeing them, they both surprisingly told me not to worry. They said that although it is true that many people have died, hemorrhaged, and even had strokes, I "had a better chance of getting hit by a bus on the way home if I was feeling nervous while crossing a street." What I had was deadly, they continued, but we had to take it day by day. I had already gone very far in life with it, which doesn't happen often. Many people born with an AVM wind up dying at birth. Others are younger than me when it is found. They explained how they work with patients with the same illness on a daily basis. Relief finally came over me and I felt I could safely place my life in their hands.

Dr. Song and my new neurologist, Dr. Mark Kupersmith helped me understand what was causing all the symptoms. They were triggered whenever the blood passing through the veins would stop due to the knot, and the knot would swell. When swollen, it would press up against my brain and cause a seizure. In my case, pressure up against my long-term memory area would bring flashbacks. I would hear voices for the same reason. The long-term memory part of my brain kept being pushed by the swelling of my veins and arteries. I had gained weight and lost my energy because my blood circulated so slowly through my heart, due to the AVM, that my metabolism slowed down and so did my energy. "Wow," I said. I could not believe it. Who would have ever thought that? They mentioned that it was surprising to them that I had not hemorrhaged already, especially after doing things like playing soccer and basketball, roller skating, gymnastics, and standing upside down during yoga.

When I broke my arm as a child, I had to take a break from gymnastics. I loved it so much that I went right back into it after my arm healed. I even did cartwheels with my cast on. My mom would go crazy seeing me do that. Unfortunately, I once again broke the same arm and the doctor said that I should no longer do gymnastics. I was very upset at that time, but it might have saved me from hemorrhaging.

Although this is something I was born with, and as mentioned, many children with an AVM die at birth, symptoms do not often arise until there is a hemorrhage or something similar. The doctors were surprised it took so long to be found.

The doctors also mentioned that had I had natural births with both my children, I would have almost definitely hemorrhaged during the first delivery. That reminded me how upset I was with my first C-section. I always wanted to have a natural birth. When I was pregnant with my second child, I asked the doctor to let me have a natural birth. I was told that if my child was not already pushing out naturally by my due date, I would need a C-section, like it or not. Thank goodness I needed the C-section. I might have lost my life at that time.

All I could think of at that time was all the moments I tried to get help from doctors and was turned away. I felt anger and disappointment at being told that I was making all this up, that there was nothing wrong with me. No one could ever understand what I went through during my life. I felt angels had always been protecting me. As I mentioned earlier, when I graduated from high school, I wanted to go to college and get a degree in speech pathology and work with American Sign Language. I started at Hudson County Community College, then Jersey City State College, then Kean College, then even Buffalo Community College. However, I still had a hard time. Now I knew why.

I thought I kept having anxiety attacks during tests, but they were seizures. I would fail with scores in the fifties. I would try to study, felt I knew all the answers, but as soon as I would have the test in front of me, I would get lightheaded, black out, and forget everything. I sometimes even had a hard time writing my name on tests because I was so faint and lost. My hand just would not write it. It felt so weird that I had no idea what was happening. I was so scared that I always wrote JMJ on the corner of my papers. That stands for Jesus, Mary, and Joseph and the sisters taught us it would assist us during tests. I kept changing colleges due to how embarrassed I felt, but could not get by. When I found out what I had, my doctor explained to me why I couldn't finish college back then. My AVM was on my frontal lobe, which controls studying, and every time I was nervous about a test, the AVM would swell. Because of the swelling, I would have a mild seizure and I would not remember anything I studied, would not be able to write my own name on the test, and I would think it was anxiety. I was always angry and scared. I always felt there was something that would keep me from studying and passing.

Chapter Ten

*M*onths later, my doctors were ready and looking forward to helping me. In January of 2006, I had my first surgery; it was endovascular, through the femoral artery, bypassing the heart, and going into the brain. The object was to fill all the veins that were feeding this malformation with onyx (crazy glue), thus killing it. The surgery went okay, and a portion of the AVM was filled, but not without a cost. I had a partial hemorrhage during my first embolization, meaning my vein ripped and there was some blood spilled on the brain. This thankfully dissipated while I was in a medically induced coma, which I had to sustain with each operation. I was kept in that state for thirty-six hours so my blood pressure could be kept within boundaries and prevent further complications. While I was in the medically induced coma, I was intubated and on a ventilator to assist with my breathing; I was heavily sedated and monitored. My family sat at the church down the block, praying for me. They were so frightened, not only for themselves, but for my children who could lose their mother.

When I awoke, an angiogram (which is full of radiation), was performed to document progress, as well as an MRI. Due to the amount of radiation, one day while brushing my hair, I realized that too much came off. I was able to extract a handful of hair by just running my fingers through it. I then went partially bald and had to get a specialized hairpiece while my hair grew back. That made it hard for me to go places and be around other people. Although the hairpiece was said to look good, I knew it wasn't my hair and was very sad. Although I had sadness within me, I was glad that the first endovascular surgery was complete.

In October of 2006, after being told that the AVM was still active and not even close to being filled or shut down, I went in for a second embolization surgery. The surgery itself went well, but the recovery did not. While in the medically induced coma, I suffered a collapsed lung because the tidal volume on the ventilator was not at the proper setting. Due to the collapsed lung, I developed pneumonia. Once again, I had a post-op angiogram, more radiation, baldness, a hairpiece, and a longer recovery at home because of the pneumonia.

In April of 2007, I underwent my third surgery. Doctors would once again attempt to fill this AVM that had become such a disturbing part of my life, but never stopped me from living it. Right before the surgery, I was told that Dr. Joon Song was no longer with Dr. Berenstein to assist with the embolization, and a new doctor would be there. His name was Dr. Rafael Ortiz. I was so scared that when I was told, I had an anxiety attack and, suddenly, I couldn't breathe. My friend at work, Antoinette, saw how I was and accompanied me to the conference room to calm me down. She then suggested I go home and relax, and she would let our manager know I had to leave for the day. Thank goodness she was there with me. When I reached home, I spoke to Dr. Berenstein's office manager, Mee Lee. She was so supportive with me. I will never forget her. She told me about Dr. Ortiz, how good a doctor he was, and that he could be trusted—and she was right. Dr. Ortiz and Dr. Berenstein worked great together.

The third surgery filled a bit more of the AVM, but because of the dangers of each operation and the amount of time the doctors were able to intrude on the brain, the entire growth was not shut down. Having all these surgeries and not being 100 percent cured really had me depressed and afraid for life. I would have nightmares at night being so afraid to be lost to my children.

In January of 2008, it was time for my fourth surgery. This one went better than the previous two, but I had a bad reaction to the pain medications and was hallucinating. I had to always have someone by my side so I would not think I was seeing dead people pass by me, or blood shooting out of my IV. I would scream in fear, saying I saw blood and was hemorrhaging. My cousin was by my side when I did that, and she went screaming for a nurse to come running in and help. When the nurse came in, she didn't see any blood, and she knew I was hallucinating. They had to cover my IV with extra bands, and my cousin had to hold my arm and hide the IV from me, so I would not see imaginary blood. When nurses with patients were passing the window of my room. I started screaming that I saw a spirit following a patient. (I do recall seeing that, but I was having a bad reaction to those meds!) That scared many patients and family members who were visiting, thinking that perhaps they were losing their loved ones in the recovery room. I felt bad once I came to and was no longer reacting to the medicine. I then waited a while longer for my fifth surgery because, at that point, I was a bit worn out.

In March of 2009, once again we were back in Saint Luke's Hospital on 59th and 10th in Manhattan. This surgery went well; however, while in the induced coma, I became more alert than I had been previously, and I attempted to pull the tube out from my throat before being sedated once again. I remember being held down while I was choking, and I thought I was going to die. Thank goodness they had control of me and quickly had me asleep. When I woke up, I was happy to know that I was alive! Not to sound like a broken record, but I had another bad reaction to the medicines that they were specifically told not to give me. Once again, I was seeing spirits and feeling like I was going to bleed to death. Thank goodness for such a strong family. They were by my side and helped me get through these times. After the surgery, again came the angiograms, MRIs, hair loss, hairpieces, and continuous recovery. Almost five years later, I am still not finished.

Years after my last embolization, I still did not feel 100 percent well. I was still dizzy at times and had headaches. After five endovascular surgeries, the doctors who performed these surgeries told me that the AVM was not completely shut off. However, to go in and attempt another endovascular surgery of that kind was way too risky, and the end result might not be favorable. They told me that the next step would be a total resection of the AVM. All the veins that sent blood to the AVM were blocked except for one on the inside of the knot of veins and arteries. I was terrified just thinking of not only losing my life, but of my children losing their mother. What if I came back and didn't remember anything? Having an open craniotomy carried great risks, but the alternative was to live every day knowing that at any given time I could have a stroke. I decided to go ahead with the surgery.

For an open brain surgery, I was sent to Dr. Saadi Ghatan. Dr. Ghatan is a genuinely nice and smart doctor. He explained everything that would go on during my AVM removal. He showed me where they would be making the incision and how I would feel upon awakening. Much of what I heard scared me. Doctors must tell you the worst just in case something were to happen. Going under was always a very scary thing to do, but this time, knowing how much different it was than an embolization, I was frightened. I made sure that I had written a letter to both my boys, letting them know how much I loved them and sharing memories of them since the day they were born. I wrote a letter to my husband at that time, my mother, sister, and brother, to let them know I loved them so much. Another thing I did was write down every password I had to certain programs. I knew I might have forgotten many things upon awakening. I also wrote myself a letter to help remind me of anything I might have lost in memory. I felt this was going to be the start of another difficult time of life.

On February 22, 2011, we were back in the hospital. This time was different because this surgery was more dangerous and much more extensive than the previous five. All I could think of were my precious boys. I had my arms around them all night telling them both how much I loved them, and that I would be okay. My mom was in tears, as they wheeled me away and brought me into the operating room. My family waited and waited and waited. The doctor saw me lying on the bed with tears falling down the sides of my face. He told me everything would be all right. At the same time, the anesthesiologist rubbed my face and said, "Goodnight Gracie," and I was asleep.

During the surgery, they had to wake me up to be sure I was still conscious. When they woke me up, I continued crying. They were able to ask me questions as they were still operating on me, and I responded well to all the questions. They were able to finish the surgery knowing I was conscious. Finally, the doctor went out and told my family the surgery was complete and all went well. However, he didn't tell them that was just the beginning.

When I finally woke up in the recovery room, I was happy to see my loved ones right by my side. Although I was conscious, as mentioned above, I was given a series of tests which were more upsetting to me than anything in my life. They asked me which hospital I was in, and I did not know. I had no idea where I was even by looking around and seeing IV tubes. I couldn't remember the day, year, month, president, or vice president; worst of all, I could not remember my own children's names or birthdays. This was too much to take and I began to cry. The doctor told me not to worry, as eventually this would all come back to me.

Slowly but surely, the memories started to come back. At first, it was still difficult because I could see the words I wanted to say in my mind, but could not make them come out of my mouth. It was as if I were suffering from aphasia. When asked questions, I knew the answer, but could not respond. That was very frustrating. Time passed, and I was happy to say that my memories were slowly returning, and I was able to speak what I saw in mind. I finally remembered my boys' names, their birthdays, and some of the bad things the boys had done in the past. (Love them ☺).

The worst part at this point, while I was still in the hospital, was the pain I was feeling. My head felt like it was pounding very strongly. At one point, I could not even open my eyes due to the pain. My mother asked friends and family to please not visit because of the pain I was in. It hurt just to hear people speaking. I was in such excruciating pain that both Dr. Berenstein and Dr. Ghatan came to see if I was okay. They performed an MRI to be sure that there was no hemorrhaging, and all looked well. The pain was not only from the incision, but I also felt that someone was in my brain and my body was trying to fight it. With the morphine, I slowly began to feel better and be more alert. I was then able to go home.

Chapter Eleven

I was grateful to finally be home, but it became very hard for me. I still had stitches on my scalp, and even after they were removed, there were other mishaps. My left eye was closed; I was unable to open or feel it. The whole left side of my face and head felt numb, and had that pins and needles feeling. I could not feel my lips on that side. If I took a drink of water, it would drip right out of my mouth. With my eye being closed, I had a hard time walking due to balance, especially when I was taking a shower or going up and down the stairs to our bedrooms.

This actually became another very scary time of my life. Patrick had to work longer night hours, and while I was home alone, I was afraid. My family was always by my side, but I felt like I could not take care of my little ones in the state I was in. I was weak and felt half-blind. If anything happened at night, I felt useless. I would not have the energy to run or pick up my little one. I started having anxiety attacks, but because my family had gone through enough with me, I didn't tell anyone. At night before bed, I would start shivering and have a hard time breathing. I would make myself go into the bathroom to put cold water on my face, but I would sometimes throw up. What if someone broke into my house? What if my child was suddenly sick and I needed to take him to the hospital at night? I prayed every night for my father's soul to please be by my side and give me strength, not only for me, but for my children.

When I started feeling better, I was able to go to a child's birthday party with my boys. Their father drove us there. It was one of the first days I spent outside in front of people, and it was not all that much fun. All eyes were on me, and all I could think of was whether food and water were sliding down the side of my mouth. The kids kept looking at me wondering, *What is wrong with that lady? Why is her eye patched up?* I was happy when we finally got home.

Six months of disability passed, but unfortunately, my eye was still not open and I was still having troubles. Because I could only be granted six months of disability, I tried to go back to work. However, it was obvious that I was not well enough. They could not take me back until I was well enough to be at a computer, among other things. They said they could not take me back without a written letter from my doctor saying all was 100 percent well. I had to stay home without pay for another six months. That made many things difficult in life.

When the year was up, although I was better, I did not feel ready for work. Nevertheless, I needed to work. We had financial difficulties because only one of us was working, and there were prior bills made with two salaries on board. I went to my doctor and asked him to please write me a letter saying I was okay to return to work. Although the letter was not 100 percent true, I did need it in order to be taken back into the corporate world.

My first week was difficult, but I had to start making a way to deal with it and help myself get by without anyone noticing my hidden disabilities. My eyes were both open, but I was having a hard time keeping my left eye open all day. Because the nerve was damaged, the eye felt very weak. I was having a hard time focusing on the computer and my sight was uneven. Looking at the computer made my eye tired, and it would close on me. I still had pins and needles and numbness in my lip on my left side. I was seeing double when I looked up or looked down.

I went to an eye doctor, who told me I would always need pyramid glasses in order to see straight. I received a pair of those glasses, which cost a lot, but the glasses were so thick. I could not start with glasses like that. I tried, but they made me feel more unbalanced and fall. How can they expect me to go from never wearing glasses to wearing a pair so thick? Therefore, I decided to live with the double vision and take care of it myself. When someone would come by me while sitting at my desk, I would look up at the person and see double. I learned that if I moved my chair back, I could see a single person instead of two.

I also had a hard time with many people around me. With groups of people on all sides of me, I had a hard time focusing. My eye would become tired and start to close. I would also get dizzy from that. Going to the mall was difficult because of the amount of people in the stores. With so many people there, I was unable to pick something out that I liked. Even today, I go to the mall early in the day, so I can focus within the stores and find something I like. Otherwise, I cannot look for a good piece of clothing to wear because I cannot see well. At work, my eye would be so tired from looking at the computer that I would have to drink lots of coffee to keep myself awake. When I walked down a flight of stairs, I needed to keep one eye closed, or I would see double staircases. For a while, I would have to hold on to the railing because I felt off-balance and was afraid of falling.

Those were just some of the issues I had when I returned to work that I still have today. I am glad that today I have been able to get used to them and live comfortably with them. Another issue was with memory. I could not remember anyone's name. I had to secretly make a sketch, which I still use today, of people's desk locations with pictures of them and their names. If I ever see someone who remembers me from a time ago, it takes me a long time to remember him or her. I always say hello as if I know who the person is, but then must investigate where I know the person from. Once I find out, then the memory comes back, and I am refreshed as to how I know that person. If not, then that person stays lost with some of my other memories.

Friends sometimes talk about instances when we were younger, but I have a hard time remembering everything that happened in my life. I spoke to an old boyfriend I had for many years, and I could hardly remember the time we spent together. It was scary and depressing that I could not remember things that I never wanted to forget. The good thing is that, as I am reminded of past instances, some start to return, and my memory snaps back. The only bad thing is that this took time.

Working a full-time job is difficult, and I can never let anyone know about the memory issues I still have today. It is funny to see how many stickies are all over my computer, but that is to help my memory. At time, when I answer the phone, I am told who I am speaking with and within just a few seconds I automatically forget. By quickly writing it, I can then remember. I also was left with aphasia, which does not help me be the person I always enjoyed being. I always liked speaking in public places and was not afraid of being in front of people. I remember being in the cast of *Romeo and Juliet* in high school. Although I couldn't remember answers for a test, I remembered all the words in a poem and lyrics from the story. I liked speaking in public. Unfortunately, since surgery, when I know what I am going to say and have it memorized, it quickly disappears, and I cannot even speak. Even when I am asked some simple thing, such as, "What department do you work in?", I can see the word in my mind, but it won't come out. When I see a manager and would love to make a good impression and be remembered for a better position, I blank out and am unable to say what I had in mind, or even answer questions in a professional and smart way. That is difficult and depressing.

Because of this, I finally went to see a speech pathologist (something I always wanted to be), and a lot of the help she provided happens to be the same kind of help I was giving myself. She gave me exercises to practice at home and things to do while I'm at work to help me remember. But I was already doing those things. I have floor plans with the names of co-workers. I have stickies on my desk to remind me of names, and so on. Aside from that, my speech pathologist is an excellent doctor, very helpful, and always at my side.

Life has been difficult over the past couple of years. Although my illness has made me lose some memory, perhaps assisted by losing a husband through divorce, as well as some of our mutual friends and even a job, I have been strong and have gotten through it. Divorce made me weak, and I felt that perhaps my surgery changed the way I am, and that helped ruin our relationship. Perhaps it made me feel that I could do better in life than live without happiness. Many of our mutual friends have unfortunately hurt me by being involved in my divorce but not caring about my suffering with heartbreak. I heard a saying once that made me feel strong and made losing some friends seem a blessing: "I pray to God to remove my enemies from my life, and before I know it, I started losing friends. Am just saying no one to be trusted," by *Meek Mill*.

Chapter Twelve

Today, I have a new job with genuinely nice people, and I am getting stronger and stronger every day. My family is always the strength in my heart. I have two beautiful sons, a mother, brother, sister-in-law, sister, nieces, nephews, aunts, and cousins who always bring out the best in me and always keep me from being hurt or afraid. My ex-husband's mother and family have also always been rocks in my life to help keep me strong. I also have friends today that I should always have had in my life.

One day, after I thought all of my illness was over with, I started feeling a little dizzy. I was also tired and weak. It wasn't the first time I had recently felt weary, dizzy, and a bit demolished. I thought that perhaps it had to do with my diet and the start of menopause. At work, sometimes I would start sweating and seeing peripheral flashes. Because I had started menopause, I blamed it for the weird feelings. I knew that going to the gym, working out, and working on being more flexible would eliminate my weakness. I once again went to my doctor, telling her I wasn't feeling too well. She had blood tests done, which showed that I needed to lower my cholesterol, and that gave one reason for the way I was feeling. I also thought that perhaps stress had a lot to do with it. My boss had been let go, and I thought I might be let go as well. I was struggling financially, and things in my house needed repair. That alone would make many people feel dizzy. Unfortunately for me, not only did it make me feel dizzy, it also caused a seizure. A seizure is something I thought I was never again going to have. I had petit mal seizures all my life, but this was a grand mal seizure my biggest fear ever.

I was on my way to the train station to drop my son at school and go to work when, suddenly, I lost attention. I don't remember almost anything after that. I became conscious for a moment and wanted to see my son to make sure he was okay. I remember seeing him and he had tears in his eyes. I held his hand, and then I was out again. I don't remember anything that followed. When I came to, I was already in the hospital. Tests were performed, but did not reveal what caused the seizure. They said perhaps stressful life situations might have caused my brain to swell and touch the scar tissue from my previous brain surgery. A person's brain swells in stress or upset; that happens to everyone. However, mine might have swollen a lot more than usual to touch my scar tissue.

I was prescribed seizure medicine again. The worst was that I could not drive for a few months. Thank goodness that my son was okay. He called 911 quickly, and then contacted his father. What made me more upset than the accident was seeing my child's face, so worried about his mother. I don't ever want to see him that upset again, or my other son, after hearing something happened to his mother.

Having that seizure not only scared me, but I feel it made me stronger. I have to stop feeling depressed about situations that happen at work, not having some friends I did in the past, or not being able to save enough money to be comfortable in life. I know that I can do better with more positives. Even my brother, while I was in the hospital, asked me to please not leave him alone in life with any of the family troubles we alone can deal with.

Many people have had what I did, and many have gone through worse. I always say a prayer for them, for they are stronger than I was. Because of the difficult times in my life, I have finally allowed myself to live strongly without fear. My children are my rock. They are my strength. I wish to be here for them, as well as other family members, always. One reason fear and sadness has been lifted is that I have always believed in angels. I feel being more connected has allowed me to enjoy life instead of always feeling depressed, unloved, and unappreciated by others aside from my family.

In addition to my five embolizations and one craniotomy, I also had gallbladder surgery, two C-sections, and two broken arms. I have gone through many strenuous situations.

One of those situations is a day I will never forget. I was in the World Trade Center on my way to work. The first plane hit on 9/11. My brother and I had arrived on the train, and while going up the stairs, we knew something had happened because everyone started running. We ran as well, and tried to leave the building. When we reached the door and tried to exit, someone screamed that we had to go back in because the sky was falling. We went back in but were pushed out by the crowd behind us, who were also trying to leave the building. Thank goodness my brother was with me, and we were able to escape and save our lives.

The sky was falling on us, but because we had each other, we found our way home. We walked through Manhattan to try to get as far away as possible. Walking uptown was scary. We were heading towards 42nd street and could see the United Nations building. We were nervous for our lives. We did not know if another building would be hit. We decided to make a left before we got any closer to the United Nations building. By then, we realized we were by Times Square—another place we felt fearful being in. If they wanted to hurt more people, that would be the place.

I remember while sitting down and taking a break from walking, a nice woman came and asked us what it was like downtown. She noticed I had glass and pieces of articles that had fallen from the World Trade Center stuck in my hair. We quickly decided to keep walking away from it all. When we got farther uptown, we found a car rental place and decided to rent a car to drive ourselves home. At that point, we were very lucky, as we were close to being one of the last cars allowed to drive over the Tapan Zee Bridge towards New Jersey.

It took us hours of sitting in traffic to get into our home town of Bayonne; it is a peninsula and the only way to enter is from Jersey City or Staten Island. The Staten Island Bridge was closed. Jersey City was not allowing anyone to enter because people from the towers were being sent out of New York City on boats entering Jersey City. We would have been on those boats later in the day had we not travelled uptown to escape the falling of the towers. We finally made it home when it was already dark. Seeing my family, especially my son (I only had one then) was the best feeling I ever felt. I still to this day thank God that we made it home.

I also thank God that my AVM didn't hemorrhage at that time as well. Amazing how things happen in life!

That, to this day, tells me there is a reason I am here. I keep getting better in life, so I can help others and fulfill my existence. Even with obstacles, my angels are always with me to assist and guide me through my journey, and I thank them always.

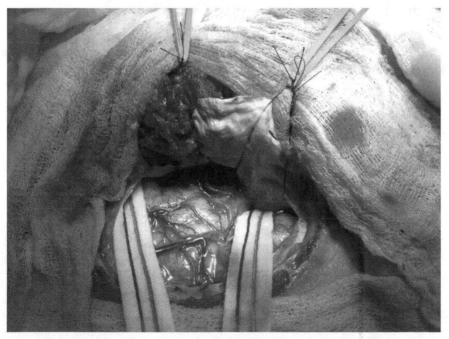

Removal of AVM

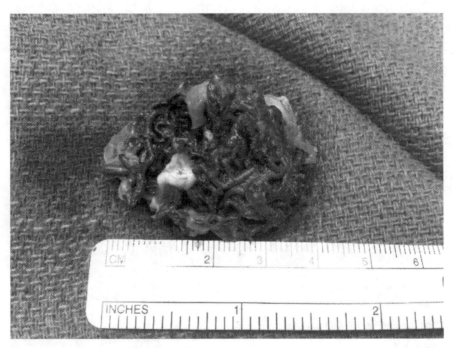

Photo of AVM once removed

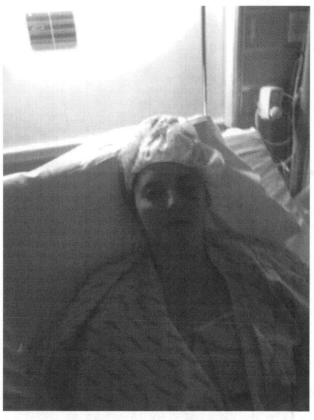

Photo of me after surgery

Printed in the United States
by Baker & Taylor Publisher Services